Brilliant Support Activities

Word Level Work – Phonics

Irene Yates

 Brilliant Publications

We hope you and your class enjoy using this book. Other books in the series include:

Language titles

Science titles

Published by Brilliant Publications
1 Church View, Sparrow Hall Farm, Edlesborough, Dunstable LU6 2ES, UK
Telephone: 01525 229720
Fax: 01525 229725
email: sales@brilliantpublications.co.uk
website: www.brilliantpublications.co.uk

Written by Irene Yates
Cover designed by Small World Design
Illustrated by Lynda Murray

Printed in the UK by Eagle Graphics (Printers) Ltd
Telephone: 01525 384893

© Irene Yates 2001
First published in 2001
ISBN 1 897675 32 1

Contents

Introduction to the series

The Brilliant Support Activities series contains four language titles designed to give reinforcement to pupils who are finding it difficult to keep up with the skills and concepts in the National Literacy Strategy. The four books are closely linked:

- Word Level Work – Vocabulary
- Word Level Work – Phonics
- Sentence Level Work
- Text Level Work

Each book contains 42 photocopiable ideas for use with Key Stage 2 pupils who are working at levels consistent with the first four years of the National Literacy Strategy document. The activities are presented in an age-appropriate manner and provide a flexible, but structured, resource for teaching pupils to understand all the concepts that are introduced in the Literacy Hour during reception, Y1, Y2 and Y3.

The tasks in the books are kept short and snappy, to facilitate concentration. The vocabulary used is especially focused on the lists of high frequency and medium frequency words that the children are to be taught as sight recognition words during the National Literacy Strategy. The pages have a clear layout and the text has been kept to a minimum so that struggling readers can cope. To ensure that the instructions are easy to follow, the following logos have been used to indicate different types of activity:

 What to do

 Think and do

 Read

 Help

Many pupils begin to feel disaffected when they find abstract language concepts hard to grasp. The activities in this series are designed, with information and questioning, to foster understanding and to help those pupils to experience success and achievement. The expectation that the pupil *will* achieve will help to build confidence, competence and self-esteem which, in turn, will foster learning.

Introduction to the book

The activity pages are designed to support and consolidate the work you do during the Literacy Hour. They are intended to add to your pupils' knowledge of how phonics work.

Some pupils have auditory discrimination or auditory memory problems. Because of this phonic rules sometimes require lots of reinforcement before they are understood. You may find that the greatest problem is the children adding the sound 'uh' to the phonemes. For example, they will say 'tuh' instead of 'tttt'. Many of the sheets in this book are designed to help to overcome this problem.

The sheets can be used with individual children, pairs or very small groups, as the need arises. The text on the pages has been kept as short as possible, so that reluctant or poorer readers will not feel swamped by 'words on the page'. For the same reason we have used white space, boxes and logos, to help the pupils to understand the sheets easily, and to give them a measure of independence in working through them.

It is not the author's intention that a teacher should expect all the children to complete all the sheets. Rather that the sheets be used with a flexible approach, so that the book will provide a bank of resources that will meet needs as they arise. Many of the sheets can be modified and extended in very simple ways.

What to do

Say the words. Write the **c**.

__ up

__ at

__ ar

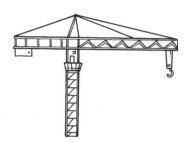

__ rane

__ omic

Think and do

Trace over the **c**'s.

C C C C C C C C C

What to do

Say the words. Write the **h**.

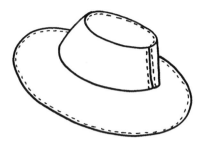

__ at

__ air

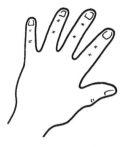

__ and

__ ippo

__ orse

Think and do

Trace over the **h**'s.

h h h h h h h h

What to do

Say the words. Write the **n**.

__ ine

__ est

__ ose

__ umbers

__ ut

Think and do

Trace over the **n**'s.

n n n n n n n n n n

What to do

Say the words. Write the **s**.

__ ad

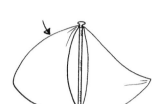

__ ail

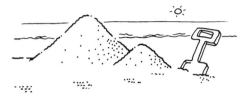

__ and

__ carf

__ ink

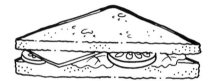

__ andwich

__ un

__ urf-board

Think and do

Trace over the **s**'s.

S S S S S S S S

What to do

Look for six words that begin with **b**.
Draw a circle round them.

get

bed dim

bad but

dip

top

bat

bin

pig bag gap

Think and do

Write in the **b**.

big   bib

bit   bob

Find the d

What to do

Look for six words that begin with **d**.
Draw a circle round them.

dad

dim

mad

pad

nip

den

dip

dab

bad

nib

bun

did

Think and do

Write in the **d**.

din

dip

day

dot

Find the m

What to do

Look for six words that begin with **m**.
Draw a circle round them.

why

me

no

my

man

mum

not

pin

map

new

win

mop

Think and do

Write in the **m**.

mop

miss

mud

mat

What to do

Look for six words that begin with **p**.
Draw a circle round them.

pot

pan   nap

dot   top

pod

tap

pen

din

pin   pat   nip

Think and do

Write in the **p**.

pit   **p**ay

pet   **p**op

Word Level Work – Phonics

Find the r

What to do

Look for six words that begin with **r**.
Draw a circle round them.

tar

rat

bit

rim

my

rub

jar

run

rag

car

pin

rug

Think and do

Write in the **r**.

ran

red

ray

rip

What to do

Look for six words that begin with **t**.
Draw a circle round them.

nut

top   tub

pit   fat

tip

ten   hen

not

yet

tap   toy

Think and do

Write in the **t**.

top   too

tea   tip

Rhymes with hen

What to do

Make a rhyme with 'en':

hen

p

d

m

t

Tick (✔) if these rhyme with *hen*:

then

when

what

Find two more words of your own:

gl

wr

Think and do

Make up a word of your own:

_ _ _ e n

What to do

Make a rhyme with 'ee':

bee

s

Tick (✔) if these rhyme with *bee*:

tea

me

sea

Find two more words of your own:

tr

thr

Think and do

Make up a word of your own:

_ _ _ e e

Word Level Work – Phonics

What to do

Make a rhyme with 'ay':

day

h

l

p

Tick (✔) if these rhyme with *day*:

    may

    hey

    by

Find three more words of your own:

    pl

    gr

    st

Think and do

Make up a word of your own:

    __ __ __ a y

What to do

Make a rhyme with 'ar':

car

f

j

b

t

Tick (✔) if these rhyme with *car*.

baa

are

bat

Make another word of your own:

st

Think and do

Make up a word of your own:

_ _ _ a r

Word Level Work – Phonics

What to do

Make a rhyme with 'ing':

king

r

s

d

w

Tick (✔) if these rhyme with *king*:

ping

pang

sting

Find three more words of your own:

br

th

cl

Think and do

Make up a word of your own:

_ _ _ i n g

Word Level Work – Phonics

This sheet may be photocopied for use by the purchasing institution only.
www.brilliantpublications.co.uk

Do these words rhyme?

Read

Words that rhyme don't always *look* the same. Sometimes they have different spellings. It is the *sound* that matters.

What to do

Draw lines to put these words into pairs.

1	pair	third
2	bricks	reach
3	bird	chair
4	found	bear
5	teach	wood
6	do	six
7	care	fear
8	be	round
9	could	meat
10	light	blue
11	here	bite
12	feet	sea

Think and do

Write your pairs here:

pair/chair

Which words rhyme?

Read
Here is a list of words:

bear

wait

fork

light

were

meal

bird

tail

hurt

eat

What to do
Write a word which rhymes at the side of each word.

Choose from these words:

wheel	whale	pork	feet	care
white	late	fur	heard	shirt

A rhyme puzzle

What to do

Read the clues. Work out the answers.

1   It is something you do with your eyes. It rhymes with *book*.   _ _ _ _

2   It is when you have spoken. It rhymes with *red*.   _ _ _ _

3   It is something you eat off. It rhymes with *eight*.   _ _ _ _ _

4   It is something you do with a spade. It rhymes with *big*.   _ _ _

5   It is something you can tell. It rhymes with *chime*.   _ _ _ _

6   It is somewhere you live. It rhymes with *dome*.   _ _ _ _

7   It is something you do with two feet. It rhymes with *hump*.   _ _ _ _

8   It is a number. It rhymes with *bee*.   _ _ _ _ _

9   It is something you do when you're happy. It rhymes with *half*.   _ _ _ _ _

10 It is something you spend. It rhymes with *honey*.   _ _ _ _ _

11 It is something you get in the post. It rhymes with *better*.   _ _ _ _ _ _

Help

Choose from these words:

plate	dig	home	jump
letter	said	time	three
money	laugh	look	

What to do

Find the words that rhyme in the lists.
Draw circles round them.

there	fair	here	care	fear
time	line	climb	mine	rhyme
fox	locks	mix	rock	socks
blow	go	blue	toe	slow
sheep	shop	keep	sleep	push
are	stare	card	star	far
back	bark	black	crack	crock
moon	spoon	mine	none	noon

Read

Say the word 'new'. Now say the word 'new' without the 'n' sound.
The sound that is left is 'ew'. Say it.

What to do

Can you make words that end with the 'ew' sound?

add the 'ew'	Write the whole word
n **ew**	new
bl	
ch	
fl	
br	
cr	
scr	
dr	
shr	
thr	
d	
f	
kn	
n	
st	

Think and do

Say your words.

Do you know the sound 'ow'?

Read

Say the word 'grow'. Now say the word 'grow' without the 'gr' sound.
The sound that is left is 'ow'. Say it.

What to do

Can you make words that end with the 'ow' sound?

add the 'ow'	Write the whole word
gr **ow**	grow
l	
bl	
sh	
sn	
fl	
thr	
cr	
m	
gl	
r	
kn	
sl	
t	
st	

Think and do

Say your words.

Do you know the sound 'y'?

Read

Say the word 'my'. Now say the word 'my' without the 'm' sound.
The sound that is left is 'y', sounding like 'igh'. Say it.

What to do

Can you make words that end with the 'y' sound?

add the 'y'	Write the whole word
b **y**	by
m	
fl	
pl	
cr	
sk	
wh	
dr	
fr	
tr	
st	
sh	

Think and do

Say your words.

Do you know the sound 'ee'?

Read

Say the word 'see'. Now say the word 'see' without the 's' sound.
The sound that is left is 'ee'. Say it.

What to do

Can you make words with the 'ee' sound?

add the 'ee'	Write the whole word
s *ee*	*see*
b	
fl	
gl	
kn	
fr	
spr	
thr	

Think and do

Say your words.

Do you know the sound 'ay'?

Read

Say the word 'say'. Now say the word 'say' without the 's' sound.
The sound that is left is 'ay'. Say it.

What to do

Can you make words that end with the 'ay' sound?

add the 'ay'	Write the whole word
d **ay**	day
m	
w	
aw	
st	
h	
p	
cl	
str	
pl	
l	
tr	
b	
sw	

Think and do

Say your words.

What to do

Can you find words to fill in the chart?

onset sound	rime sound							
	ad	am	an	ap	at	ell	en	et
b						bell		bet
c								
d								
f								
g				gap				
h								
j								
l	lad							
m								

Think and do

How many words have you made?

This sheet may be photocopied for use by the purchasing institution only.
www.brilliantpublications.co.uk

What to do

Can you find words to fill in the chart?

onset sound	rime sound						
	ill	in	ip	op	ot	ug	ash
b							bash
c							
d							
f	fill						
g							
h			hip				
j					jot		
l							
m							

Think and do

How many words have you made?

What to do

Can you find words to fill in the chart?

onset sound	rime sound							
	ad	am	an	ap	at	ell	en	et
n								
p	pad							
r			ran					
s								
t						tell		
w								
sh								
th							then	
ch								

Think and do

How many words have you made?

Word Level Work – Phonics

What to do

Can you find words to fill in the chart?

onset sound	rime sound						
	ill	in	ip	op	ot	ug	ash
n			nip				
p							
r					rot		
s							
t							
w	will						
sh			ship				
th							
ch							

Think and do

How many words have you made?

Beginning sounds 1

Read

Read these words. Notice the sound at the beginning of each word:

dry	black	brick
cream	blue	drive
brave	dwell	crack
dwindle	click	clumsy

What to do

Put each word into its group. Write one more word for each group.

bl	br	cl	cr	dr	dw

Help

Say the beginning clusters aloud.

Word Level Work – Phonics

Beginning sounds 2

Read

Read these words. Notice the sound at the beginning of each word:

flag	glass	frame
pretty	glide	play
please	frog	grim
flicker	grass	prince

What to do

Put each word into its group. Write one more word for each group.

fl	fr	gl	gr	pl	pr

Help

Say the beginning clusters aloud.

Read

Read these words. Notice the sound at the beginning of each word:

skid

scare

scrub

spin

slip

snap

scatter

snow

scream

skip

smash

smile

spill

slide

What to do

Put each word into its group. Write one more word for each group.

sc	scr	sk	sl	sm	sn	sp

Help

Say the beginning clusters aloud.

Read

Read these words. Notice the sound at the beginning of each word:

squint	spring	star
splutter	switch	stripe
splash	square	stair
stream	swing	spray

What to do

Put each word into its group. Write one more word for each group.

spl	spr	squ	st	str	sw

Help

Say the beginning clusters aloud.

Read

Read these words. Notice the sound at the beginning of each word:

shrub

track

throat

trip

three

shrug

twirl

twin

What to do

Put each word into its group. Write one more word for each group.

tr	tw	thr	shr

Help

Say the beginning clusters aloud.

Read

Say the word 'will'. Now say the word 'will' without the 'wi' sound.
The end sound is 'll'. Say it.

What to do

Draw a circle round the words that end with the 'll' sound.

bell	bowl
silk	shell
fill	drill
meal	feel
spell	well
tell	milk
still	told
rule	bull
bail	bill
trail	chill

Think and do

How many words have you found?

_____

Help

The 'll' sound does not always *look* the same at the end of a word.

Words ending with 'mp'

Read

Say the word 'bump'. Now say the word 'bump' without the 'bu' sound.
The end sound is 'mp'. Say it.

What to do

Find words that end with 'mp'.

amp	imp	ump
lamp	chimp	lump

Think and do

How many words have you found? _____

Which vowel sound has the most? _____

Words ending with 'nt'

Read

Say the word 'went'. Now say the word 'went' without the 'we' sound.
The end sound is 'nt'. Say it.

What to do

Find words that end with 'nt'.

ant	ent	int	oint
rant	went	tint	point

Think and do

How many words have you found? _____

Which vowel sound has the most? _____

Words ending with `nd`

Read

Say the word 'and'. Now say the word 'and' without the 'a' sound.
The end sound is 'nd'. Say it.

What to do

Find words that end with 'nd'.

and	end	ind	ond	ound
hand	bend	kind	fond	pound

Think and do

How many words have you found? _____

Which vowel sound has the most? _____

This sheet may be photocopied for use by the purchasing institution only.
www.brilliantpublications.co.uk

What to do

Look at the words carefully. Say them.
Draw a circle round the words that end with the 'nk' sound.

think

teeth

blink

thank

kick

sink

nick

shrunk

pink

drink

cling

sing

junk

bunk

think

dunk

keen

clink

clunk

string

Think and do

How many words did you find?
Write them here:

What to do

Look at the words carefully. Say them.
Draw a circle round the words that end with the 'st' sound.

list

stop

dressed

mast

waste

stem

fist

chest

mist

fast

crest

stay

nest

last

best

twist

past

stitch

stiff

vest

Think and do

How many words did you find?
Write them here:

Help

The 'st' sound does not always *look* the same at the end of a word.

Word Level Work – Phonics

This sheet may be photocopied for use by the purchasing institution only.
www.brilliantpublications.co.uk

What to do

Look at the words carefully. Say them.
Draw a circle round the words that end with the 'sk' sound.

skip   bask

disk

whisk   packs

gonk

rusk

kips

risk   brisk

sank

sulk

lick

tusk

junk

mask   task

chunk   dusk

skunk

Think and do

How many words did you find?
Write them here:

Sounds like 'ff'

What to do

Look at the words carefully. Say them.
Draw a circle round the words that end with the 'ff' sound.

foe   tiff

off   if   puff

cliff

elf

stuff   tug

scruff   fluff

foot

biff

stiff

gruff   fit

feel   file

shelf

self

Think and do

How many words did you find?
Write them here:

Help

The 'ff' sound does not always *look* the same at the end of a word.

This sheet may be photocopied for use by the purchasing institution only.
www.brilliantpublications.co.uk

What to do

Look at the words carefully. Say them.
Draw a circle round the words that end with the 'ng' sound.

ring

nag

big

bang

green   wing

glean

spring   niggle

blink

bag

clang   kind

gone

king

gleam

again

sing

song

bring

Think and do

How many words did you find?
Write them here:

Sounds like 'ck'

What to do

Look at the words carefully. Say them.
Draw a circle round the words that end with the 'ck' sound.

rock

stitch

wreck

block

back

rich

dish

switch

dash

knock

clock

match

click

king

knit

sock

thick

deck

Think and do

How many words did you find?
Write them here: